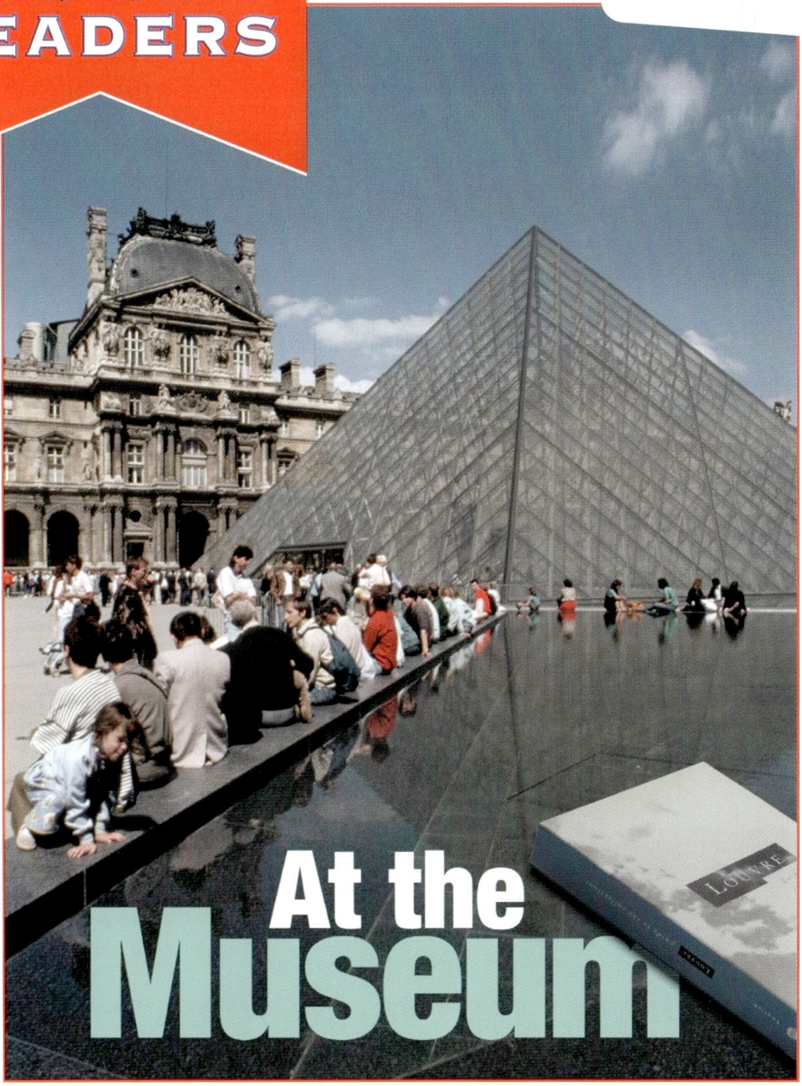

At the Museum

by Jeri Cipriano

Harcourt

Orlando   Austin   Chicago   New York   Toronto   London   San Diego

Visit *The Learning Site!*
www.harcourtschool.com

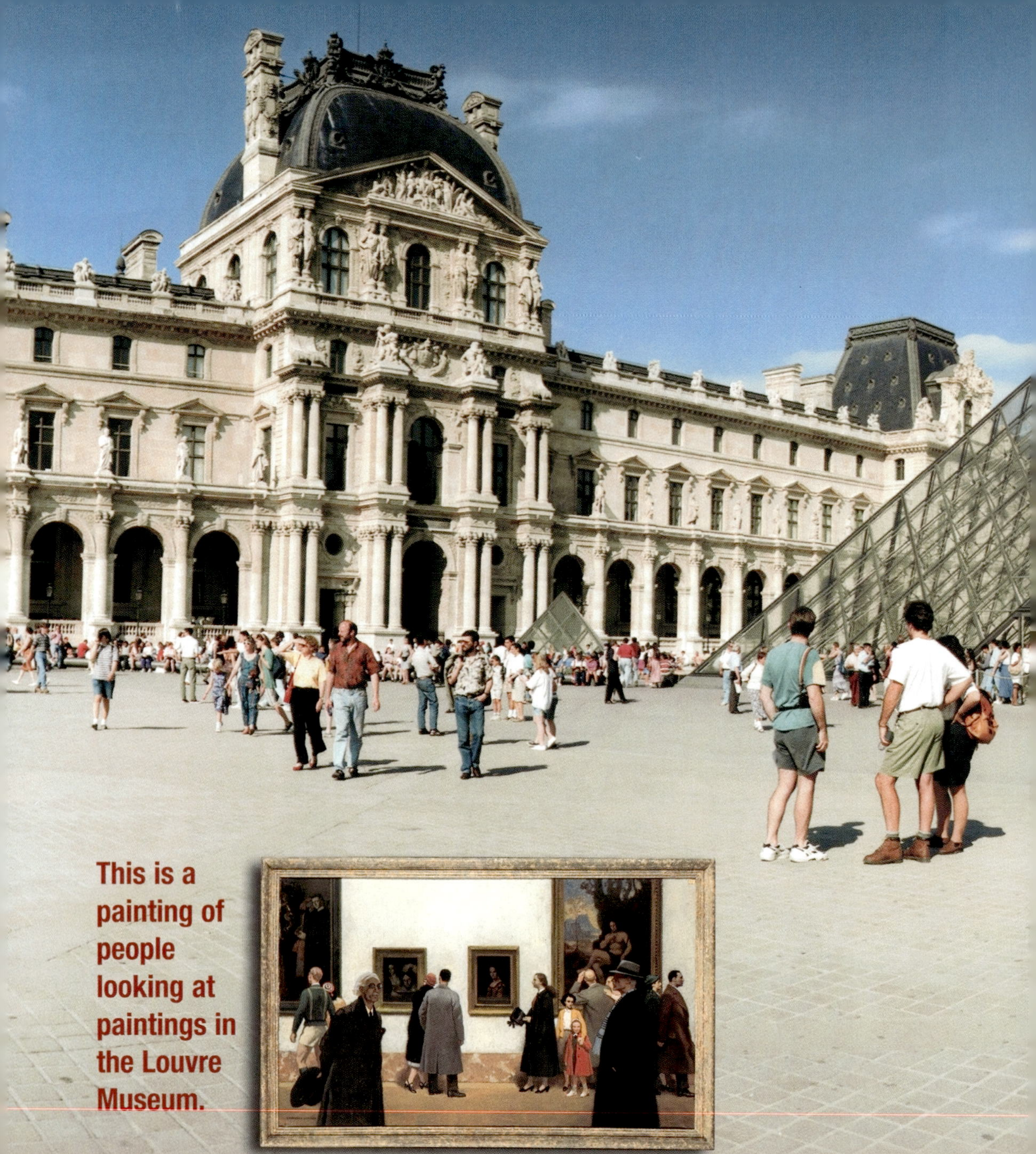

People like to visit museums. They go to see beautiful art. They look at paintings, sculptures, and objects from long ago.

The Louvre is a famous museum in Paris, France. The museum itself is a work of art. One of its buildings was once a palace where kings lived!

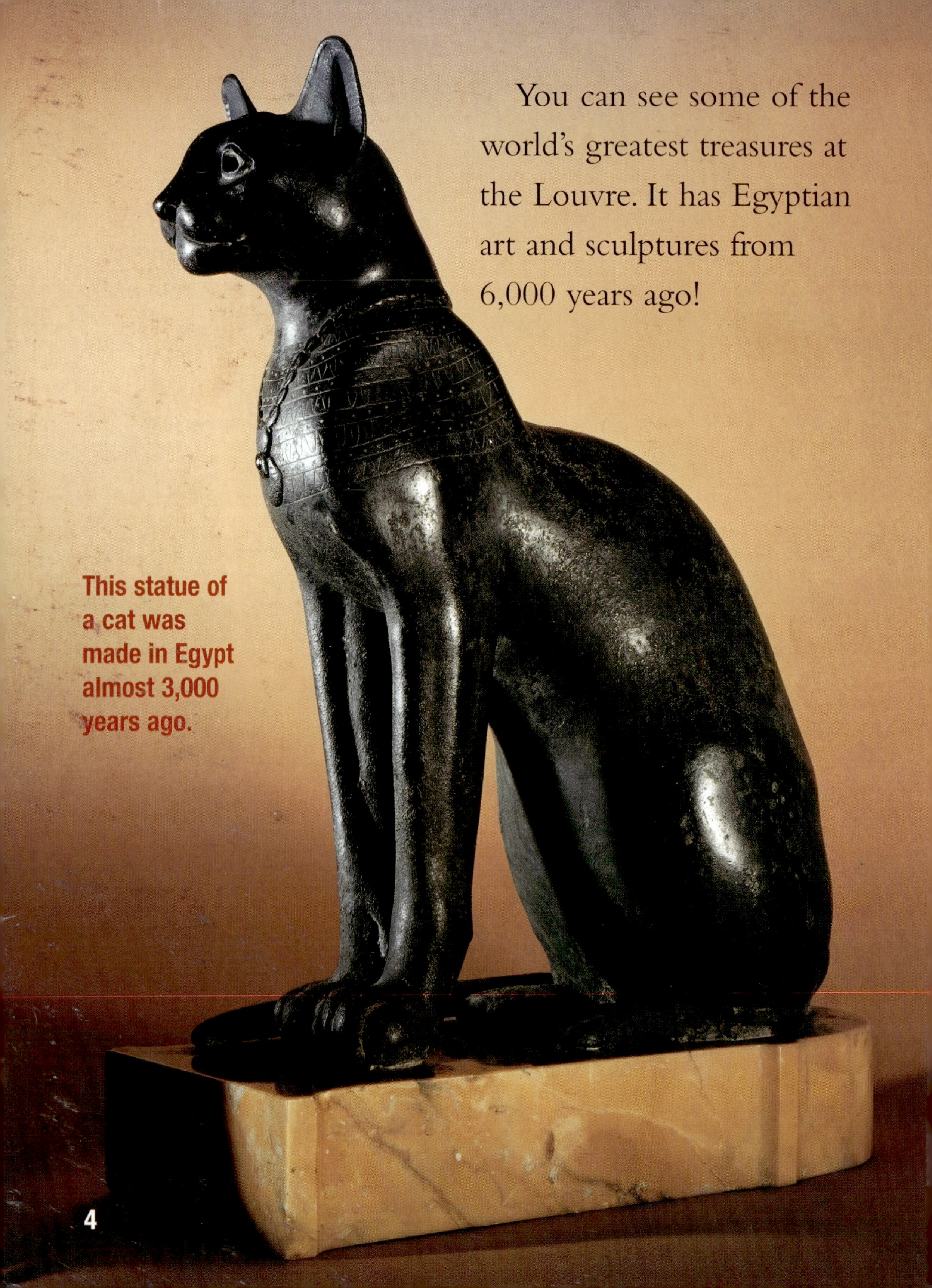

You can see some of the world's greatest treasures at the Louvre. It has Egyptian art and sculptures from 6,000 years ago!

This statue of a cat was made in Egypt almost 3,000 years ago.

The Louvre has statues
and objects from ancient
Greece and Rome. It
also has art from other
early cultures.

An ancient Greek vase
shows women dancing.

This French chair
was probably made
in the 1700s.

The Mona Lisa was painted by Leonardo da Vinci.

The Louvre has more than 6,000 European paintings. This portrait of an Italian woman was painted in 1503. Some say the woman is smiling. What do you think?

The Louvre has art by some of the world's greatest artists, such as Jan Vermeer. At the Louvre, you can see paintings that are hundreds of years old.